SUMMARY

------ ❧❧❦❧❧ ------

12 Rules for Life

An Antidote to Chaos

Book by
Jordan B. Petersen

FastDigest-Summary

© Copyright 2018 - Present.
All rights reserved.

This document is geared towards providing reliable information in regards to the topic and issue covered. The publication is sold with the idea that the publisher is not required to render accounting, officially permitted, or otherwise, qualified services. If advice is necessary, legal, or professional, a practiced individual in the profession shall be ordered.

— From a Declaration of Principles which was accepted and approved equally by a Committee of the American Bar Association and a Committee of Publishers and Associations.

In no way is it legal to reproduce, duplicate, or transmit any part of this document in either electronic means or in printed format. Recording of this publication is strictly prohibited and any storage of this document is not allowed unless with written permission from the publisher. All rights reserved.

The information provided herein is stated to be truthful and consistent, in that any liability, in terms of inattention or otherwise, by any usage or abuse of any policies, processes, or directions contained within is solely and completely the responsibility of the recipient reader. Under no circumstances will any legal responsibility or blame be held against the publisher for any reparation, damages, or monetary loss due to the information herein, either directly or indirectly.

Respective authors own all copyrights not held by the publisher.

Before we proceed...

Feel free to follow us on social media to be notified of future summaries.

1- *Facebook: BookSummaries*

https://www.facebook.com/BookSummaries-1060732983986564/

2- *Instagram: BookSummaries*

https://www.instagram.com/booksummaries/

TABLE OF CONTENTS

INTRODUCTION 1

SUMMARY 3

    PART 1: THE ABILITY OF STANDING UP STRAIGHT ... 3

PART 2: WE NEED TO CONSTANTLY HELP OURSELVES AND WE SHOULD TREAT OURSELVES THAT WAY 5

    PART 3: CAREFULLY CHOOSE PEOPLE YOU WANT TO BE FRIENDS WITH 7

    PART 4: ALWAYS COMPARE YOURSELF WHAT AND WHO YOU WERE YESTERDAY 9

    PART 5: IT IS IMPORTANT TO RAISE THE CHILDREN IN A "PROPER" WAY 11

PART 6: CLEAN YOUR OWN YARD FIRST BEFORE STARTING TO CRITICIZE THE WORLD 13

    PART 7: WE NEED TO PURSUE WHAT TRULY MATTERS 15

PART 8: TELLING THE TRUTH AND BEING HONEST IS ONE OF THE MOST IMPORTANT ASPECTS OF LIFE 17

    PART 9: PEOPLE MIGHT KNOW A LOT MORE THAN WE DO 19

PART 10: SAY WHAT YOU WANT TO SAY IN A PRECISE WAY 21

PART 11: LEAVE THE CHILDREN ALONE WHEN THEY ARE SKATEBOARDING 23

    PART 12: BE GOOD AND ACT GOOD TOWARD PEOPLE WHO ARE DIFFERENT FROM YOU 25

ANALYSIS	27
QUIZ	29
QUIZ ANSWERS	33
CONCLUSION	35

INTRODUCTION

Welcome to the 12 Rules for Life book summary! This summary is not the original book. However, if you like the summary, please purchase the original book for full content!

12 Rules for Life: An Antidote to Chaos is a self—help and bestselling book written by Dr. Jordan Petersen. Dr. Petersen is a clinical psychologist and psychology professor, which is one of the most important reasons why he decided to write this book.

Some of the most important things the author discusses in his book are abstract principles about life in general and the influence of biology and other subjects, such as religion, myth, and the author's professional experience. When compared to his previous work *Maps of Meaning: The Architecture of Belief*, 12 Rules for Life is written in a much more reader—friendly and accessible style of writing, which is definitely a good thing, both for the author and for readers.

This summary will be divided into several parts. The first part—the introduction serves as a short intro of the book. The second part—the summary—will be the largest and the most detailed part, because it will contain much information and details from the original book. After the summary, there is a book analysis, where we will analyze some of the key points from the book. A quiz with its answers will be the part of the

12 RULES FOR LIFE

summary where our readers will have the opportunity to test everything they learned about the book from the summary section. The last part will be the conclusion of the book. If you are ready, please proceed to the summary section. Enjoy!

SUMMARY

PART 1:
THE ABILITY OF STANDING UP STRAIGHT

Dr. Petersen opens his book and its first chapter by writing about lobsters and their "perception" of territory. The author deduces that the lobsters are in many ways similar to humans when it comes to most basic "ways" of behavior. For example, when it comes to territory, lobsters react somewhat similarly to how humans react. The author says that lobsters, regardless of the fact that they exist in something Dr. Petersen calls the "deeper sphere" have their own way of creating their safe areas. Moreover, lobsters also have their own ways to fight for their existence.

The second part of the chapter is about how birds perceive their territory. Here the author writes about similarities and differences when it comes to birds and lobsters when it comes to territory.

Dr. Petersen observed how the birds defend their territory by watching the actions of a wren. A wren came to the author's birdhouse. After she came, that wren did not allow other birds to come in the area where she was. Moreover, that same wren attacked the author on one occasion. This happened when the author played a birdsong on a recorder.

12 RULES FOR LIFE

The wren wanted to show to every other bird (and everyone else) that she is the ruler of the territory where she currently was.

The thing with the lobsters is that they also fight for their territory. Often, their fight will last until they lose their life.

After these two examples, the author writes about the states of winning and losing. He states that there is a chemical factor found in the body of the animals. Serotonin is a factor that will keep the individual happy and mighty, thus helping the subject to win. The next thing the author writes about is the Matthew Principle. This principle dictates that people who win in many different things will keep winning and that those who keep losing will continue that trend. What this principle says is that it is the "losing attitude" that prevents people from winning.

The same is with male/female relationships, where the female decides to stick with whoever is the most "alpha" male in the group (or in a society). When it comes to survival, the author states that being the fittest and the strongest means that they have good confidence in the outcome. When we perceive things positively there is a far better chance that we will succeed, even though things do not look so good. When we are down, there is a big possibility that we will fail in what we do because of our perception of our situation and ourselves.

PART 2:
WE NEED TO CONSTANTLY HELP OURSELVES AND WE SHOULD TREAT OURSELVES THAT WAY

At the beginning of this chapter, the author wonders why humans in general care less for themselves but are willing to help others if necessary. After this, the author writes that there are three things that "create" the world of humans—the order, the chaos, and the human consciousness. Therefore, humans tend to follow the element of subjectivity around and everything that looks predictable will remain the same. If a human can rely on something, he will call that the order. However, if something is "out of order" and if something corrupts the serenity and peace—that is called the chaos.

The next thing the author writes about is the story of Adam and Eve in the Garden of Eden. He describes how the snake (or Satan, the fallen angel) seduced the woman by offering her the apple. Then the author describes the fall of men from his psychological perspective. At the end of this part of the chapter the author deduces that because humans overlook the mistakes of others, while their own remain their highlight, humans want to help others rather than helping themselves.

12 RULES FOR LIFE

The next part of the chapter is about the human perception of good and evil. The author states that this perception is something that was given to humans by God. This perception of good and evil also helps humans to see the good in others. However, even though we are bound to help others because, as the author states, we see the good in others, the author still cannot deduce why humans still do not want to help themselves.

Humans still fail to understand that they are just important as others around them (or animals or any other thing/object/creature they love).

PART 3:
CAREFULLY CHOOSE PEOPLE YOU WANT TO BE FRIENDS WITH

The third chapter starts with the author describing the town of Fairview, Alberta and its citizens. Since there was no Internet or video games, the townspeople spent great deal of their time socializing. Then the author writes about his friend Chris and his cousin Ed. They both were a source of interest to the author since the author could never understand why Chris, although a genius, was never happy. As we read the chapter, we learn that the main reason Chris was so unhappy and unsuccessful was that he did not have faith that things would turn out for the better. The author thus learned that there is a particular joy in having good friends; they can make the best out of us and make us want to become better—both as persons and in our professional lives.

At the end of the chapter, the author writes his definition of friendship. He states that a friendship is a type of a relationship in which two persons want what is best for each other. If one person in that relationship does not want to see the best and to do the best for other person, that relationship will be flawed and there will be difficulties in maintaining it. It is beneficial for us to find friends who will push us forward. Friends who will want only what is best for us will help us in the long run.

PART 4:
ALWAYS COMPARE YOURSELF WHAT AND WHO YOU WERE YESTERDAY

There will always be someone better than we are. This is just how things are. When we see someone rising, we may feel unappreciated and simply—inferior. However, things are often not as simple as they may seem. Thus, it is wrong to compare and to succumb to this.

We often think that we need to be the best we possibly can in everything there is in life. We think that we need to achieve as much as possible if we want to be perceived as successful. That is not how things should be. We humans often do not see things how they really are. For example, when we see someone who is happy and smiling, we tend to think that that person is always happy and that he does not have any problems. However, that is often not the whole picture. Many times, we only see one fragment of the whole. Because of that, we tend to become jealous of others. We think that they are "better than we are" and that they have something that "belongs to us."

When it comes to the days that are in front of us, one very important thing we should do is to take small steps or small changes each day. One small change can, and eventually will, lead towards bigger changes. We may not see them at the beginning, but they will become more and more visible with time.

People often tend to focus their attention on trying to solve problems and situations, which are either too difficult or not possible for us to solve. This can lead to disappointment. Often, happiness is something a lot more important than victory.

PART 5:
IT IS IMPORTANT TO RAISE THE CHILDREN IN A "PROPER" WAY

In this chapter, the author writes about raising children and how can parents have control over the outcome of their children's actions. Furthermore, the author states that the first years of a child's life are crucial when it comes to forming them. Discipline is vital, both for parents and for children. Properly disciplined children will bring order in life, while negatively disciplined children would later bring chaos.

One thing that every parent should consider a top priority when it comes to children is mannerisms. However, many parents fail in discovering what mannerism means. Thus, many parents allow their children to enjoy too great freedom, which later leads to chaos, anarchy, and bad habits. It is easy to develop bad habits. However, an effort is required (both from parents and children) to develop good habits.

When it comes to disciplining children, sometimes parents will need to utilize a small bit of force. This force should never lead to violence. Instead, every forceful action should be utilized in moderation. Its purpose should be only for teaching the importance of obeying the authority and rules.

When considering the rules, the author states that a parent should not keep a big list of rules. That can be counterproductive. Instead, a parent should keep small, doable, and easy to understand rules. Later the author emphasizes the importance of a child having two parents rather than just one.

PART 6:
CLEAN YOUR OWN YARD FIRST BEFORE STARTING TO CRITICIZE THE WORLD

The sixth chapter starts with the author's claims that suffering is a part of life and that people should not immediately connect suffering and problems with religious elements. Suffering can influence us in two different ways: we can hold a grudge against a person (or a situation) and become vengeful, or we can forgive and move on. Unfortunately, there are many examples of people holding grudges against others. These people often want to have their revenge. However, being vengeful is not beneficial for us. It is harmful for us, because revenge makes us as much evil as the people who wronged us. When we decide to forgive and to move on, that liberates us and gives us freedom over the situation and a person. Vengeance and negative emotions trap us in a vicious cycle. However, forgiveness gives us freedom over everything that wanted to keep us chained in one place.

Besides other people and situations, we can cause our own suffering. For example, when we fail to do something we ought to do, because we were forgetful, or negligent, we can suffer. Instead of blaming destiny, God, or others for our failure, we should instead embrace the responsibility that lies in us.

Another thing we should stop doing is highlighting the faults and mistakes of others. Instead of finding fault in others, we should constantly evaluate ourselves and improve ourselves in every possible way.

PART 7:
WE NEED TO PURSUE WHAT TRULY MATTERS

Our life will eventually end. We are here for a limited time. Thus, we should invest the time that we have into things that truly matter. We should live our lives in order to accomplish the very best possible.

When it comes to money and financial resources, the author also puts a lot of emphasis on the importance of saving. When we save, we can have enough money to can keep us from financial troubles in the future.

When it comes to evil and the suffering in the world, these have been present since the beginning of the world. The key—important thing—here is trying not to succumb to evil or the devil. That is why we should strive to forgive and never become vengeful, because that will make us bringers of suffering.

People are sinful creatures. We constantly engage in sin. What can prevent us from acting in sin is that we understand the nature of our actions before we act. Think before you act. This can save you a lot of trouble and can prevent many bad things from happening, both to you and to others around you.

PART 8:
TELLING THE TRUTH AND BEING HONEST IS ONE OF THE MOST IMPORTANT ASPECTS OF LIFE

Here the author gives his own explanation why telling the truth is far better and more beneficial, both for us and for others, than telling lies.

A lie is and often will be, harmful and hurtful. However, the truth, although it may seem different, will always bring us freedom. Later in the chapter, the author describes his example and further explains the importance of telling the truth, both to ourselves and to others. Telling the truth can save our relationships from many problems that could occur if we choose not to tell the truth or tell a lie.

Another thing very important when talking about truth is the importance of living a life filled with truths. Living a "false life" will bring suffering to us. When we fabricate something just to show to others how good and successful we are (when, in fact we are not), our lives will go on in circles. Things will "return back to us" until we learn the lesson. This is why it looks as if many people are constantly "stuck" in one place: because they often *are* stuck in one place. Living a fabricated, false life will never bring any good to us.

PART 9:
PEOPLE MIGHT KNOW A LOT MORE THAN WE DO

We often give advices to others, because we often want to help them. However, giving advice to someone negates the possibility that that person maybe know more than we do.

When it comes to thinking about everything, it is good for us to have someone to think with us, someone we can share our ideas and opinions with fearlessly. That way we can know better if what we think, or what we think we know, is good or bad.

When it comes to listening others, the important thing here is to listen completely without prejudice. This is something that therapists especially should keep in mind. Listening is a crucial part of communication, because when listening, we can learn many things we did not know. Moreover, many things we assumed when we did not listen could be changed. When having a conversation with someone, it is very important to have a dialogue and not a monologue. Actively listen what other person says, ask sub-questions and pay attention to what they are saying. Do not assume. Listen.

PART 10:
SAY WHAT YOU WANT TO SAY IN A PRECISE WAY

This chapter opens with the author's deduction that everything in life goes through an evolution. Things that matter now will be substituted with things that are more important in the future.

Our views on something (or everything we are involved with) are very important to all of us. Being involved matters to us and becomes important to us.

When our connections with others become destroyed or compromised, we tend to blame one factor. However, often are several factors that are responsible for the situation at hand.

Our lives can be difficult because difficult things may happen. Relationships can break, friendships can break, and people may die. We may lose our jobs. Things can get rough. However, in order for us to heal and to move on, the first thing we have to do is to accept the situation. We also need to discover what caused the issue and what caused the situation. This can help us to deal with an issue in a far better way.

PART 11: LEAVE THE CHILDREN ALONE WHEN THEY ARE SKATEBOARDING

The author starts this chapter by saying that people want to be excited one way or another. Moreover, people want continually to switch between things that cause the excitement.

When it comes to taking correct or false paths, every time we take a correct path we will know it. A correct path will eventually lead us to true success and to improved, better versions of ourselves.

In the second part of the chapter, Dr. Petersen writes about our conditions as human beings. He states that our condition as human beings has worsened because we constantly judge other people and things around us. Instead of trying to improve ourselves, we tend to judge others and see flaws on and within them, which eventually leads to the deterioration of our societies.

At the end of this chapter, the author deduces that men also need to have some female traits. One of these traits is the ability to better interact with others (which includes active listening and listening in general). Instead of being overly aggressive, boys and men should strive for other ways of showing their masculinity.

PART 12:
BE GOOD AND ACT GOOD TOWARD PEOPLE WHO ARE DIFFERENT FROM YOU

Every one of us has his or her favorites. These favorites usually share some (or most) of our traits, characteristics and qualities. However, in our lives we often come across people who are different from us. Even though it is sometimes difficult to love these people, loving them and being good to them is beneficial for us. Diversities are important in our lives. They make us grow even more and make us better in so many ways.

When a problem occurs in our life, it is easy only to look on the problem. However, if we want to win, we should not allow our problems to keep us at bay for too long. Instead, we should actively search for solutions for our problems. Every time we face a problem or a challenge, we should also look around and try to find positive things that we have. That way we will make our problem-solving and success-achieving paths a lot easier.

ANALYSIS

1 2 Rules for Life: An Antidote to Chaos is a self-help book written by an author with clear understanding about the matter. Dr. Petersen is an expert in psychology, which is something we can see immediately after we open the book and start reading it. This is definitely a positive thing, because it makes everything the book is about and everything the author writes about much more authentic.

When it comes to writing style, the book is written in a combination of two styles. We can see that the author did everything he could in order to write his book in a reader-friendly way. This means that the author wanted to make this book available for everyone, regardless of age and education. However, when reading the book one cannot but notice that, although there are many reader-friendly elements included, the book also has that "professional tone of voice." The sentences are structured in a way that it sometimes can be a problem to follow what the author wanted to say. This happens especially between the chapters, when the author wants to say something new or when he wants to explain his next rule. Regardless of that, the writing style of the author will not keep readers from finishing the book and from understanding everything the author wanted to say.

As for the chapter length analysis, the chapters are not too short or too long. This is surely a positive thing, because it makes following the book a lot easier. Every chapter holds one rule (out of twelve) and every chapter is divided into several sub-chapters. This again makes following the book a lot easier.

QUIZ

Welcome to our short quiz! In this quiz, our readers will have the opportunity to put everything they have learned about the book to the test. The questions are easy to answer and short. If you are ready, please proceed to question number one. Good luck!

QUESTION 1

The book you were reading about was about certain rules of life. How many rules did the author mention in his book?

    a) Seventeen rules.

    b) Fifteen rules.

    (c) Twelve rules.

    d) Eleven rules.

QUESTION 2

What is the name of the author of this book?

    a) Jordan D. Petersen.

    b) Jordan A. Petersen.

    c) Jackson B. Petersen.

12 RULES FOR LIFE

(d) Jordan B. Petersen.

QUESTION 3

"Another thing that is very important when talking about truth is the importance of living a life filled with truths. Living a "false life" will bring suffering to us."

FALSE   (TRUE)

QUESTION 4

What did the author say is the most important when it comes to listening to others?

   a) We should actively listen to what other person is saying.

   b) We should pay attention what others say when they speak to us.

   c) We should never interrupt others when speaking.

   (d) Everything above is true.

QUESTION 5

"Dr. Petersen observed how __the birds__ defend their territory by watching the actions of a __wren__."

QUIZ

QUESTION 6

"The author states that a friendship is a type of a relationship in which two persons want what is best for each other."

(TRUE) FALSE

QUESTION 7

"People often tend to focus their attention into trying to _solve problems_ and situations, which are either _too difficult_ or not possible for us to solve. This can lead towards _disappointments_."

QUESTION 8

What did the author write about solving the problems? What should we do when we encounter a problem and what is what we should not do?

a) When encountering a problem we should immediately try to find the solution for it.

b) When a problem occurs we should try to solve it and if we cannot we should ask for help.

(c) When a problem occurs, the first thing we should do is that we should try to discover the source of the problem. That will enable much easier for us to solve it.

d) Nothing from above.

QUIZ ANSWERS

QUESTION 1–c

QUESTION 2–d

QUESTION 3–TRUE

QUESTION 4–d

QUESTION 5–"the birds, wren."

QUESTION 6–TRUE

QUESTION 7–"solve problems, too difficult, disappointment."

QUESTION 8–c

CONCLUSION

12 Rules for Life: An Antidote to Chaos is a book in which we can find interesting advice about our minds, physical health, relationships, friendships, religion, and a practical approach to problem-solving situations in our lives and about life in general. Its author, Dr. Jordan B. Petersen, an expert in psychology, wanted to show his readers his opinions on many important segments of our lives. Thus, he decided to write a self-help book where we can read a lot of practical and truly useful advice that can help us in life.

Since this is a summary of the original book, it does not contain everything the original book contains. If you like the summary, please purchase the original book.

Thank You and more...

Thank you for taking the time to read this book. I hope you've gained some knowledge about the ***12 Rules for Life.***

There are many other individuals to whom information about ***12 Rules for Life,*** will be just as useful, so I would greatly appreciate it if you post a good review on Amazon Kindle where you purchased this book and share it on social media (Facebook, Instagram, etc.), it will help others obtain this knowledge as well.

I would greatly appreciate it!

www.amazon.com

FURTHER READINGS

If you are interested in other book summaries, feel free to check out the summaries below.

1- Summary–Mindset: The New Psychology of Success
https://www.amazon.com/dp/B078MV4S93/

2- Summary–Good to Great
https://www.amazon.com//dp/B078H4CMB9/

3- Summary–The Nightingale
https://www.amazon.com/dp/B078RV7XQQ/

4- Summary–StrengthsFinder 2.0
https://www.amazon.com/dp/B078R4N79W/

5- Summary–Getting Things Done
https://www.amazon.com//dp/B078YPTN8S/

To find other book summaries, click the link below:

https://www.amazon.com/s/ref=nb_sb_noss?url=search—alias%3Daps&field—keywords=fastdigest+summary

Made in the USA
Middletown, DE
31 July 2018